DRAKE

Gareth Stevens
Publishing

By Robert Kennedy

Please visit our website, www.garethstevens.com. For a free color catalog of all our high-quality books, call toll free 1-800-542-2595 or fax 1-877-542-2596.

Library of Congress Cataloging-in-Publication Data

Kennedy, Robert (Robert Shea)
Drake / Robert Kennedy.
    p. cm. — (Hip-hop headliners)
Includes index.
ISBN 978-1-4339-6606-4 (pbk.)
ISBN 978-1-4339-6607-1 (6-pack)
ISBN 978-1-4339-6604-0 (library binding)
1. Drake, 1986—Juvenile literature. 2. Rap musicians—United States—Juvenile literature.
I. Title.
ML3930.D73K46 2012
782.421649092—dc23
[B]
                                2011019607

First Edition

Published in 2012 by
Gareth Stevens Publishing
111 East 14th Street, Suite 349
New York, NY 10003

Designer: Haley W. Harasymiw
Editor: Therese M. Shea

Photo credits: Cover background Shutterstock.com; cover, p. 1 (Drake) Robyn Beck/Getty Images; p. 5 Frazer Harrison/Getty Images; pp. 7, 19 Kevin Winter/Getty Images; pp. 9, 11, 27 Frederick M. Brown/Getty Images; p. 13 Christopher Polk/Getty Images; pp. 15, 25 Jason Merritt/Getty Images; p. 17 Amanda Edwards/Getty Images; p. 21 Tim Mosenfelder/Getty Images; p. 23 Kevin Mazur/Getty Images; p. 29 Jag Gundu/Getty Images.

Printed in the United States of America

CPSIA compliance information: Batch #CW12GS: For further information contact Gareth Stevens, New York, New York at 1-800-542-2595.

Contents

Twice a Star

Drake is a hip-hop star. Sometimes he is called Drizzy. He was a TV actor first. At that time, he was known as Aubrey Graham. Drake has a lot of names and a lot of talent!

Musical Family

Drake was born October 24, 1986. His full name is Aubrey Drake Graham. He grew up in the city of Toronto in Ontario, Canada.

Drake's father is a drummer. Drake has uncles who are musicians, too. He grew up loving different kinds of music.

Drake's parents divorced when he was 5. He lived most of the year in Toronto with his mother. He spent some summers with his father in Memphis, Tennessee.

Big Break

Drake studied acting in high school. He had a friend whose father was a talent agent. His friend told his father about Drake. The man wanted to be Drake's agent!

Drake tried out for many roles. His first parts were in commercials. Then, in 2001, Drake began acting on a Canadian TV show called *Degrassi: The Next Generation*.

Drake played a high school basketball star on *Degrassi*. In 2002, he was honored for his acting. Drake starred on *Degrassi* until 2009.

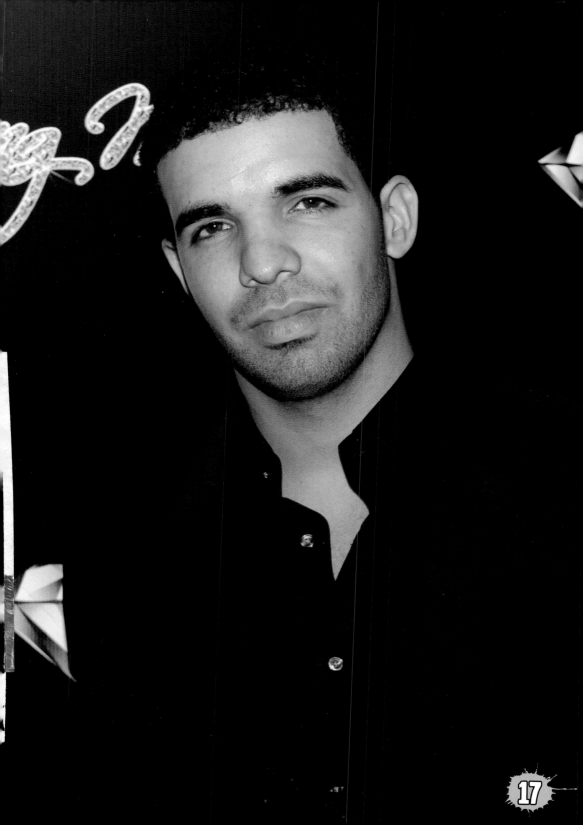

The Move to Music

While Drake was acting, he was writing rap music. In 2006, he made recordings of his music called mixtapes. Many people in the music business heard Drake's mixtapes.

Drake worked with hip-hop star Trey Songz on a song called "Replacement Girl." In 2007, the song was played on TV. Even more people heard Drake's music.

Soon everyone was talking about the young rapper. Jay-Z, Kanye West, and Lil Wayne said they loved his music.

Jay-Z

In 2009, Drake's song "Best I Ever Had" reached number 2 on the music charts. Drake began working with a record company.

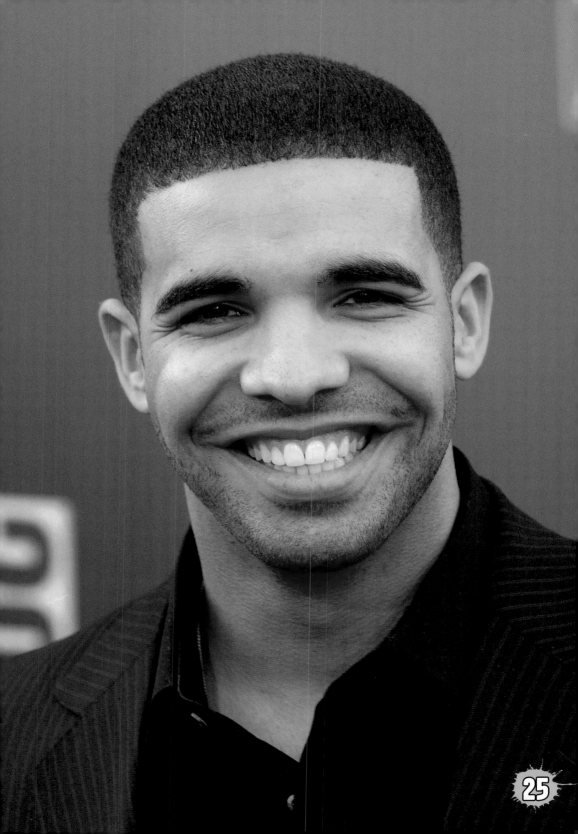

Chart Topper

In 2010, Drake put out his first album. It was called *Thank Me Later*. It reached number 1 on the first day! Drake won Best New Artist and Rap Recording of the Year.

Drake worked on his second album right away. *Take Care* came out in 2011. He also acted in movies. Drizzy Drake plans to stay a busy hip-hop star!

Timeline

1986   Aubrey Drake Graham is born in Toronto, Canada.

2001   Drake begins his role on *Degrassi: The Next Generation*.

2006   Drake puts out his first mixtape.

2007   "Replacement Girl" is played on TV.

2009   "Best I Ever Had" comes out. Drake's role on *Degrassi* ends.

2010   *Thank Me Later* comes out.

2011   *Take Care* comes out.

For More Information

Books

Cornish, Melanie J. *The History of Hip Hop*. New York, NY: Crabtree Publishing, 2009.

Earl, C.F. *Drake*. Philadelphia, PA: Mason Crest, 2012.

Websites

Drake

www.billboard.com/artist/drake/855020
See how Drake's music is climbing the charts.

Drake Official

www.drakeofficial.com
Read about Drake's life on his website.

Glossary

commercial: a way of selling goods or services on TV or radio

divorce: to end a marriage

musician: one who plays, makes, or sings music

recording: a copy of music or other sounds

talent agent: one who helps an actor or musician find work

Index